AQÜITÍN

ENVIRONMENTAL EDUCATIONAL MAGAZINE
OF WATER AND NATURE FOR CHILDREN.

SPECIAL EDITION FRIENDS OF NATURE

AUTHOR: YOLANDA MARÍA. JORGE BESTEIRO
ILLUSTRATOR: EDUARDO REYES ESCUDERO

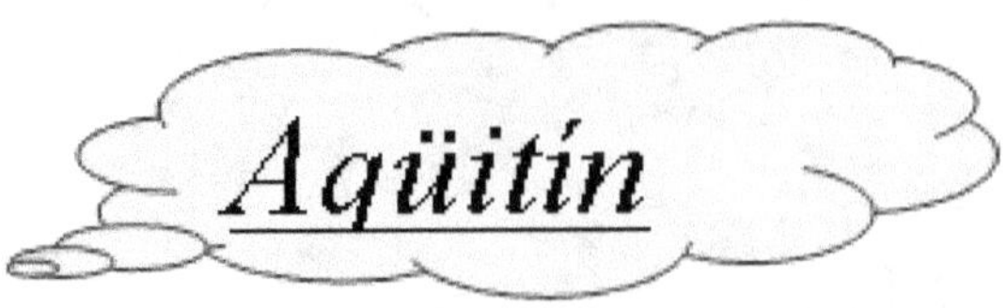

Special Edition in commemoration of several important anniversaries in our Magazine.

- March 3rd World Wildlife Day.

- March 21st, World Forest Day and World Poetry Day (a literary genre that accompanies us and identifies us as an Educational Magazine that bets on the integral teaching of Nature sciences using Literature).

- March 22nd, World Water Day, a special date that gives its name to our magazine AQÜITÍN, which comes from AQÜA in Latin.

- 7 April, World Health Day, which is intimately linked to the health of the Environment.

- April 22 International Mother Earth Day.

- April 23rd International Book Day

ACKNOWLEDGMENTS

-To my dear friend Doctor Ernesto Kahan, always willing to offer us his literary creation, and this time giving us, besides a beautiful poem, an exclusive painting of his authorship for our readers, children and young people.
Beloved Doctor of Peace, know that, in this Environmental Educational Magazine for the children of the world, your works will always be considered as a beautiful legacy from you to the new generations.

-To each of the writers, poets and teachers who have collaborated as Friends of Nature in this special edition by sending their work from other continents, thank you very much. And infinite thanks for the effort and dedication of the teachers who work daily with the children on the themes of our magazine and politely send me photos, images, drawings, etc. of the students. Thank you for instilling these values in them, and know that we recognize your work, without you we would not be effective from the magazine.

-Special thanks to my dear friend Lic María Cristina Azcona for her beautiful poem and her hard work for Culture and Peace by bringing together writers and poets.

-Eternal gratitude to my dear friend and colleague in favor of mother tongues, myths and American legends, Gladys Mercedes Acevedo for her timely vignette of Artemito and the beautiful story and illustration, and we reiterate her as a collaborator of the Magazine.

-I appreciate the generosity of the painters who offered us their beautiful works on nature, from our magazine we are eternally grateful. They are contributing with their collaboration to encourage readers in this precious art. They say that a picture says more than a thousand words. Thank you, once again.

-Thanks to the children for their works and because all the effort we make in the magazine would be meaningless without them, to whom are dedicated every story, poem, cartoon, drawing and painting that we publish in this special edition and throughout the year in the remaining editions of AQÜITÍN.

We hope that every child and young reader will make them their own in their lives, in their schools and families and spread them everywhere so that they can learn and teach others to protect forests, water, flora, fauna and nature in general.

As we also celebrate the day of poetry declared by UNESCO on March 21, we promote from AQÜITÍN the linguistic diversity through poetic expression. So, we take this opportunity to honor all the participating poets for promoting the reading, writing and teaching of poetry, and to encourage the convergence between literary creation and other arts such as painting and music.

FROM OUR MAGAZINE AQÜITÍN THANK YOU FOREVER, TO ALL OF YOU FRIENDS OF NATURE.

Yolanda María Jorge Besteiro
Lic Biochemistry University of Havana Degree Homologated in Spain E.U. 2003.
Master of Science MsC Water Engineering / MsC Plant Physiology-Biochemistry.
Social and Health Care Technician.
Scientific Disseminator-Writer. Poet. Essayist. Historian.
Professor of Biology Successworld Academy Hispanic Biology 1
Ambassador of the International Association of Hispanic American Poets and Writers AIPEH Orlando Fl USA
Cultural Ambassador of the United Nations of Letters and Manager of Seeds of Youth in Spain.
Cultural Ambassador Spain World Association of Latin American Writers
Ambassador World Wide Peace Organization Sevilla
Cultural Ambassador Cultural Ambassador International Chamber of Writers and Artists Barcelona
Honorary Member of the Literature of Peace Forum IFLAC Seville
M H World Union of Poets for Peace and Freedom UMPPL Brescia Italy

AQUITIN

Section 1

IMPORTANCE OF FORESTS

The COVID-19 pandemic has taught us that forest loss and degradation is one of the factors that contribute to disrupting the balance of nature and increasing the risk and exposure to zoonotic diseases, those caused by microbes of animal origin.

Malaria, Ebola, Zika, dengue fever, Lyme disease are all associated with the alteration and loss of habitats due to forest land use change.

<u>FORESTS. WONDERFUL SHIELDS AGAINST VIRUSES.</u>

Forests are home to most of the planet's biodiversity. They are the habitat of 80% of amphibian species, 75% of bird species and 68% of mammal species.

They have a protective effect due to the abundance of biodiversity against the spread of viruses. Unaltered natural systems reduce the possible transmission of diseases, as pathogens are diluted among the diversity of species, thus limiting or even blocking their spread.

Changes in land use and the destruction of natural habitats, such as tropical forests, are considered to be responsible for at least half of the emerging zoonoses. In addition to the disappearance of species, this reality brings people and farm animals into direct contact with animal species they have never approached before, and with it the diseases they may harbor.

Studies show that the decline of some wild animal populations may favor the explosion of others, such as small rodents, which are well adapted to ecosystems altered by humans, with a considerable viral load.

Forests act as a flood barrier.

Deforestation is an evil that we have to stop, the rate of net forest loss decreased in the last decade, also 4.6 million hectares of forest have been lost per year, according to the State of the World's Forests report presented in the summer by the United Nations, an organization that also warns that there are still 25 years to go to reach the goal of ending deforestation, a commitment that should have been fulfilled in 2020.

DID YOU KNOW THAT WE DEPEND ON FORESTS?

- 70% of the atmospheric humidity generated in terrestrial areas comes from them.

- More than 75% of the world's crops depend on pollinators that live in forested areas.

- One billion people directly seek their food from them. They are key to climate mitigation and adaptation.

- They filter air and water, act as a barrier to flooding.

- They reduce soil erosion.

- They create microclimates.

Painting Dr. Ernesto Kahan 2019 Acrylic on canvas 90cm x 70 cm. Offered to the children for this Special Edition in Homage to the Forests.

I asked the millenary trees about grass and our planet Earth.

Poems excerpted from the collection of poems:
Kahan, Ernesto. Ante réquiem and En Camino, pages 21, 25 and
29. Ed Dunken 2012 Buenos Aires

After the light was separated from the darkness
and the waters became sweetly sweet,
the darkness came back and dried up the waters
the waters and weeps the greenness of the grass.
Sorrow for the abandoned seed-grass,
sorrow for the old tree
and awaits death, life.
Woe to the pollutants!
Alas for the ecology!
Alas for the future!
O man!
Bless you!
Mother grass
Bless you!
Searching for the secrets
in the tree of the new fruit
of mother grass
Bless you!

Children's choir
do not close the door
before our passing
Free be
the water for the springs
for the courses and the plants
Free be
to walk along the road
to gather the perfumes for the butterflies

<u>**BEST ALLIES IN THE FACE OF CLIMATE CHANGE**</u>

By protecting forests and oceans from pollution, we would be preserving the most natural and effective method of absorbing and sequestering CO2. Their capacity is extraordinary.

There are estimates that establish that a tree stores an average of 22 kilos of CO2 per year.

Tropical rainforests retain 250 billion tons of carbon dioxide in trees alone, equivalent to 90 years of global emissions.

European forests sequester approximately 10% of the total greenhouse gases emitted by the European Union.

 In Spain, forests sequester one ton of carbon per hectare per year.

According to the Food and Agriculture Organization of the United Nations, deforestation is the second most important cause of climate change (the first is the burning of fossil fuels).

WE HAVE TO DO SOMETHING TO CHANGE THE MENTALITY OF GOVERNMENTS AND SOCIETY.

So that they understand that forests and trees in general make an essential contribution to the health of the planet.

Three quarters of the planet's accessible freshwater comes from forested watersheds (forests that keep losing and losing trees).

We propose that on this International Day of Forests, although we cannot go out of our homes for long distances because of the pandemic of the coronavirus and take a bath of them, try to become aware of the importance they have in your life and in the lives of your loved ones.

In eastern Ecuador, belonging to the Amazon, the wildest area of the country, an immense region and one of the least altered on the planet, very few human beings live.

Almost all of them belong to indigenous peoples under threat of extinction, such as the Achuar, the Secoya, the Shuar, the Siona, the Huaorani or the Zaparo, who struggle to preserve their traditional way of life in the face of the temptations (and pressures) of modern life.

But the real wealth of the region is its overwhelming biodiversity.

The jungle's interior is home to 50% of the country's mammals and 5% of the Earth's plant species.

Travelers can reach the most remote jungle refuges, fish for piranhas in silent lakes, hear the menacing cry of howler monkeys, see the glowing eyes of the caiman at night, admire colorful parrots feasting and, with luck, catch a glimpse of a large mammal such as a tapir or jaguar. But this region is not only jungle: it also offers the best thermal baths in the country, the most spectacular waterfall, the most active volcanoes and formidable white waters.

Section 2

IMPORTANCE OF BIODIVERSITY IN NATURE.

The coronavirus outbreak represents an enormous risk to public health and the global economy, but also to biodiversity. However, biodiversity can be part of the solution, as a diversity of species makes it difficult for pathogens to spread rapidly.

This Mother Earth Day, coinciding with the Super Year of Biodiversity, focuses on the role of biodiversity as an indicator of Earth's health.

Equally, its impact on human health is increasingly evident. Changes in biodiversity affect the functioning of ecosystems and can lead to significant alterations in the goods and services they provide. Specific links between health and biodiversity include potential impacts on nutrition, health research and traditional medicine, the generation of new infectious diseases, and significant changes in the distribution of plants, pathogens, animals and even human settlements, which may be encouraged by climate change.

Despite current efforts, biodiversity is deteriorating worldwide at a rate unprecedented in human history. It is estimated that around one million animal and plant species are currently at risk of extinction.

With this big picture and coronavirus scenario, our immediate priority is to prevent the spread of COVID-19, but in the long term, it is important to address habitat and biodiversity loss.

We are in this fight together with our Mother Earth.

ARTEMITO JOINS THE FRIENDS OF NATURE.

Because you miss the men and want them back?

Why the trees are wearing masks?

What can we tell these majestic creatures about their trees, their spaces, their forests?

They have the right to be respected, they also want to raise their children and live-in peace with the beautiful nature that surrounds them. Why don't we learn to live together in harmony? The planet belongs to everyone, each creature has a space and yes, we can all live together, respecting each other and protecting the most vulnerable. LET'S MAKE THE PLANET A BETTER WORLD

Mother Earth clearly asks us to act. Nature is suffering. The fires in Australia, the highest terrestrial heat records and the worst locust invasion in Kenya.... Now we are facing COVID -19, a global health pandemic with a strong link to the health of our ecosystem.

Climate change, human-induced changes in nature, as well as crimes that disrupt biodiversity, such as deforestation, land-use change, intensive agricultural and livestock production or the growing illegal wildlife trade, can increase contact and transmission of infectious diseases from animals to humans (zoonotic diseases).

According to UNEP (United Nations Environment Program), a new infectious disease emerges in humans every 4 months. Of these diseases, 75% come from animals. This shows the close relationship between human, animal and environmental health.

The visible and positive impact of the virus, whether through improved air quality or reduced greenhouse gas emissions, is only temporary, as it is due to the tragic economic slowdown and human distress.

Let us remember International Mother Earth Day April 22, we need a shift to a more sustainable economy that works for both people and planet. Let us promote harmony with nature and the Earth.

"Amazon soul fibers"

Yolanda Ma Jorge Besteiro

American Amazon

Biodiversity in its purest state

Refuges in your jungles

More than earthly, celestial creatures

With hot springs and waterfalls

Volcanoes and white waters

You shelter from the cruel darkness

of this world to those who love you

Indigenous people that palpitate in your jungle lungs

Sionas, Achuar, redwoods, Huaorani, Zaparos

Who with their lives recall the footsteps

Of the ancestors of America

Incas, Mayas and Aztecs

Who fluttered like eagles

and roamed the Andean altiplanos.

You hide in your forests

Living jungle full of energy

You overflow passion in the hearts

Of the wild beasts that hide

behind the greenery of your plants

Create new life and threatened offspring

That only under your cover will endure into tomorrow.

Waterfall Salto de Eyipantla Rainforest Veracruz Mexico

Acrylic on canvas Dandelion

Squirrel monkey South American jungle. Colored pencil

Elephant. Pointillism on paper and India ink.

**Eduardo Reyes Escudero Profesor y Pintor Muralista. México.
Autor de la Obra de Portada de esta Edición Especial en Fusión
Digital.**

A Refuge on the Lake (Velatura on canvas) 2020.

Pigment with oil 1999

Photography

Three beautiful works of Manuel Garrocho Escobar Mural Painter and Photographer Seville Spain.

As a curiosity and for your knowledge the World Wildlife Day March 3 of each year is celebrated only since 2013.

Date proclaimed by the General Assembly of the United Nations, as a commemoration of the Anniversary of the adoption in 1973 of the Convention on International Trade in Endangered Species of Wild Fauna and Flora.

Another reason why tougher law are needed is because man plunders ecosystems, kills for pleasure, kidnaps to sell and profit from innocent creatures that outside their habitats, if they survive, are condemned to death.

And the flora in the same way, if we use pesticides and pesticides with toxic chemicals we annihilate the target species for which the pesticide was prepared, but also with many others, which are necessary for the function of pollination, essential for the reproduction of plants and without them there is no propagation of seeds.

In addition to eroding the soil, many small animals that live in the soil, such as worms, earthworms, among many others, die because of this cause, as well as the microorganisms and microbiota that live on the soil surface, on which the plants feed and vice versa.

LEARNING MORE ABOUT ANIMALS AND THEIR CHARACTERISTICS.

Introducing the beautiful Praying Mantis.

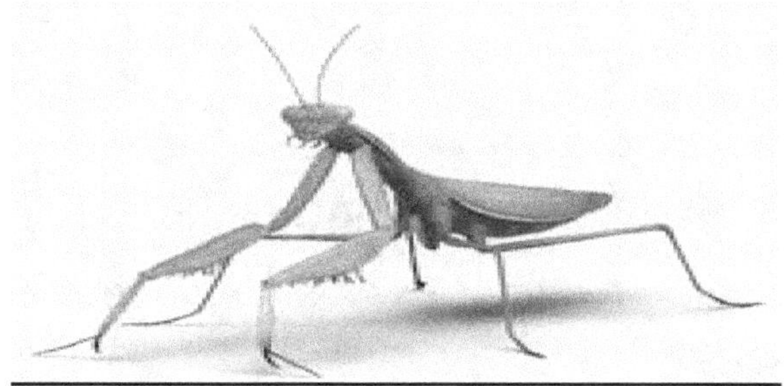

If you're out and about this time of year, you may encounter one of the world's most intriguing insects: praying mantises. Despite their serrated arms and alien eyes, they pose no threat unless you're an insect, gecko or hummingbird.

Sydney Brannoch, a mantis expert at the Cleveland Museum of Natural History, explains that praying mantises in the Americas are always around, only apparently, they are more abundant in late summer and fall, becoming more visible because, among other things, it's mating season.

This voracious insect feeds on frogs, lizards, salamanders, newts, shrews, mice, snakes, small soft-shelled turtles and even a small bat on one occasion and small hummingbirds.

Clearly these insects are voracious predators, but .... Can praying mantises harm a human?

It is very unlikely. Praying mantises are not venomous and cannot sting. They also do not carry infectious diseases.

Although some varieties such as the East African species Leptocoloa phthisica can reach 25 centimeters in length, they have rather small mouths.

They are charismatic and beautiful animals, and we have much to discover about them, so if you come across these curious creatures, do not harm them or allow others to harm them. Many children use to hunt insects and lizards to use them as suet for spiders and snakes. Don't do it, taking them out of their habitats depresses, stresses and kills them. They are of great help to man wherever they are found. This article was originally published on nationalgeographic.com.

If you are tired of your plants being nibbled by insects, and they are too many to kill by hand or too small to see, releasing a praying mantis in your garden is the solution.

Without using pesticides, mantids will keep those destructive insects under control.

We will be able to say goodbye to cockroaches, flies and mosquitoes, beetles, grasshoppers and the pesky aphids that are hard to see.

But be careful not to overdo it, farmers recommend not to have a multitude of mantids in the orchard, as they devour all insects, whether invasive or beneficial. They have a large size, but you can see that they do not harm humans, so don't harm them either.

<u>**Animals that live in forests:**</u>

<u>1. Brown bear</u>

The brown bear, or Ursus arctos, is a huge forest animal with a thick, thick and robust coat of brown, cream and even black.

Its strong paws move large rocks and its small eyes have a color similar to its fur.

Despite its fierce carnivore-like appearance, the grizzly bear is an omnivore, feeding almost entirely on plants and fruits, although it uses its large jaw and huge claws to defend itself against predators.

It inhabits the forests of North America, Europe and Asia and hibernates during the winter season.

2. Owl

The owl (Bubo bubo) is a mostly nocturnal animal characterized by its sharp vision and large size, reaching 1.7 meters in length when it expands its wings.

It is considered the most intelligent bird in the world and lives up to 60 years.

As for its appearance, the owl has large eyes protected by three eyelids, as well as abundant plumage of various shades and 14 vertebrae in its neck that allow it to rotate it at a 360-degree angle.

It is an animal that lives in temperate forests and semi-desert areas.

The jaguar, or Panthera onca, is another of the animals that live in the forest that you should know.

It is a feline found only in the forests of the American continent, where it has become one of the dominant predators.

It is a carnivorous animal and catches its prey with its huge claws and strong jaw, capable of tearing through almost anything.

It is a very solitary animal, except during mating season. It has 2 to 4 offspring per litter and these remain with their mother until they are two years old.

4. Raccoon

The raccoon (Procyon cancrivorus) is a forest animal that lives near rivers. Its fur is gray on the back, with white shades on the legs and dark stripes on the tail.

In addition, it has a kind of dark mask around its eyes. It is an omnivorous animal, feeding on fruits, vegetables, frogs and small insects.

It prefers the night to catch its prey, as it has excellent eyesight.

It is also a solitary animal and forms short bonds when it comes to having offspring, since males interact with them for little more than a month.

5. Giant panda

The giant panda, or Ailuropoda melanoleuca, is a temperate forest animal characterized by its black and white fur, making it special to the eye.

It has an excellent sense of hearing and smell, but its vision is poor.

They measure up to 1 meter 80 centimeters and weigh 150 kilograms, and their favorite food is bamboo, which represents almost the totality of their diet, although some also consume small insects and even mice.

They are very calm and sleep almost all day long in the temperate forests where they live.

6. Tiger

The tiger (Panthera tigris) is considered the largest feline in the world.

It is very agile and has great abilities, possessing excellent vision to identify its prey at great distances, even at night. In addition, it can swim and capture its prey in the water.

It is carnivorous and its main prey are deer, buffalo, crocodiles, fish, birds, reptiles and even bears.

It is a territorial mammal, so it attacks immediately if it detects any intruder. It is an animal that lives in the forests and grasslands of East and Southeast Asia.

<u>**7. Deer**</u>

The deer, or Cervus elaphus, is a mammal that inhabits mixed forests, although it is also found in valleys and cold areas such as the Arctic.

It is characterized by its enormous antlers made of bone, which it uses to mark territory and defend itself from other animals, although they do not leave mortal wounds.

The deer's body has strong and flexible limbs, as well as long legs that allow it to move in the terrain.

It feeds on leaves, bark and grasses.

The lynx (Lynx rufus) is a feline that inhabits European forests. Most bobcats have white fur on the chest, abdomen and thighs. Their tails are short, they have long whiskers, and they have black feathers on the tips of their ears, which allow them to hear better. Its tail is small, compared to other felines, measuring between 2 and 6 inches.

It is carnivorous and hunts using its large claws; its main prey are deer, birds, hares and fish, as they are excellent swimmers. The lynx is not a fast runner, so it uses ambush and silent surprise to catch its prey. They live up to 15 years in the wild and 25 years in captivity.

9. Woodpecker

The woodpecker, or Colaptes melanochloros, is a bird with a long beak that it uses to bore into tree trunks and different wood surfaces in order to extract all kinds of insects.

It is known as woodpecker all over the world because the sound it makes when pecking trees is loud and resembles a hammer hitting the wood.

Its plumage is black with shades of white, brown and green, in addition to a characteristic red crest.

The woodpecker is one of the animals that live in temperate forests with large trees.

10. Gorilla

The gorilla (Troglodytes gorilla) is a dark-furred primate that inhabits the coastal forests of the African continent. Males weigh up to 190 kilograms and are 2 meters tall, while females are 1.6 meters tall and weigh about 90 kilograms.

Gorillas have strong and long limbs, the upper ones being much larger than the lower ones.

They are very intelligent animals and use tools for feeding, sticks and small stones. They feed on fruits and leaves.

11. Tasmanian devil

The Tasmanian devil, or Sarcophilus harrisii, is a small marsupial that inhabits the dark forests of Tasmania.

It is characterized by emitting a loud screech that can be heard several kilometers away, as well as small eyes and sharp teeth that made the first settlers call it "demon".

It has nocturnal habits and is carnivorous. It feeds on carrion, although it occasionally eats some fruits or plants.

Despite its small size, it is a very dexterous animal, as it climbs tree branches easily and quickly.

12. Wood frog

The wood frog (Lithobates sylvaticus) is a small amphibian only 51 millimeters long.

It is an animal that lives in forests and wetlands where freshwater is prevalent. Its body can be dark brown, black or green.

The wood frog is extremophilic, which means that it withstands low temperatures to the limit of freezing and surviving.

As soon as it comes out of this freezing stage, it looks for a mate to reproduce. It feeds on all kinds of insects that it catches with its tongue.

Section 4 Get informed and updated.

According to information published in the press by UNEP, there are 31 countries that totally lack access to clean water sources.

One out of every four people does not have access to clean water and more than five million people die every year from contaminated water.

Therefore, from Aqüitín we invite all readers, children and young people from their homes, schools and institutes to collaborate in this sense to save water and teach their parents that you educate by example.

We want to count on the support of all of you who will continue this work in the future and will inherit our deficiencies. That is why we need everyone.

Nature needs us and now is not the time to postpone this task.

In the 1st issue of Aqüitín we told you what a tsunami was and about its consequences in India.

We keep you informed of the events that continue to occur after the tragedy occurred there and the problems that are being generated through water where the floods caused by the tsunami in India the main threat is stagnant water.

"Standing water can be as deadly as moving water," said UNICEF Executive Director Carol Bellamy yesterday.

"Flooding has contaminated water systems, leaving people with few options except to use contaminated surface water. Under these conditions, people have a very difficult time protecting themselves from cholera, diarrhea and other deadly diseases."

Children, who make up at least one-third of the total population in the worst-affected countries, are especially vulnerable to waterborne diseases.

Water purification tablets and oral rehydration salts to combat diarrhea are part of UNICEF's first shipment to the worst-affected areas of Sri Lanka.

Contamination of drinking water sources and overburdened health care services can lead to the spread of disease.

Affected children in the tsunami zone have diseases that are directly related to the prevention and treatment of malaria, diseases related to lack of safe drinking water (cholera, dysentery, diarrhea), measles, tetanus and respiratory diseases.

Malaria and dengue are epidemics that, in the current situation, with stagnant water, favor the reproduction of these mosquitoes.

CHILDREN WRITERS, POETS AND ILLUSTRATORS

"THE GOODNESS OF NATURE".

Ángely Tatiana Bernal Quintero. Pupiales Colombia (7 years old).

At her young age she is a recognized National and International award-winning Declamadora.

How I would begin my story, once upon a time....

In a far away country... I think so, I like this beginning.

In a far way country, called Colombia and more exactly in a very small town where I live, Ángely.

I am 7 years old; I am in the second year of primary school; I love reading stories and narrations; they are fun and transport me to fantastic worlds.

And with this story I want other children like me to know my beautiful town.

It is called Pupiales and my grandmother explained to me that it is in the south of Colombia and we have Ecuador as a neighboring country.

Well, it is a small town full of small houses, there are no buildings like in the cities; the biggest thing I look at, are its two temples that I look at them as two giants.

Around the houses there is a lot of nature, corn, potatoes, peas and vegetables and especially many trees, flowers and mountains; that is why butterflies and birds have their homes here.

When I go for a walk on a sunny day I like to listen to the sounds and songs of the birds and run after the beautiful butterflies.

What a beautiful paradise, where I can be free in the green meadows and enjoy the scent of the countryside...

Picking flowers of so many colors, lying down and looking at the sky and discovering so many figures of little animals in the clouds of the sky, shouting out loud that I love all this and I know that the goodness of nature will act in favor of us human beings and we will enjoy it again without fear.

She is inviting us again to be part of her greatness, taking care of her and loving her forever.

"CRYSTAL DROPLETS".

Ángely Taliana B. Quintero Country. Colombia Age. 7 years old.

With amazement I look at the sky
when a cloud starts shouting,
There they go, there they go!
those precious crystal droplets.

Collect them in a bowl,
this precious liquid,
Collect it with love,
the plants thank you
and the birds alike.

Oh, precious crystal droplets,
that give to the earth,
Life and Happiness.

El árbol gigante

Había una vez un lindo jardín, con verde follage y variedad de frutos, allí vivian muchos animales

Por el jardin pasaba una pequeña corriente de agua, que nacía de un árbol gigante, quien cuidaba aquel árbol era una tranquila tortuga, que siempre compartia el valioso líquido.

Un dia el leon se apodero del árbol, para ser dueño del agua y todos clamaran su ayuda.

Todos los animales tenian mucha séd, la tierra ya no daba frutos y unas plantas comenzaron a marchitarse y otras murieron.

Uno a uno fueron los animales a rogarle al león que compartiera el agua, pero todo fue imposible.

lo tortuga que era la mas sabia de todos aconsejo: que se deberían unir para lograr tener el agua.

El Loro con su astucia logro distraer al leon, mientras los demas derribaron el árbol al tiempo, el arbol comenzo a tambalearse y arroja grandes gotas de agua. No aguantando más la fuerza de los animales, el árbol cayo, y algunas ramas quedaron en el cielo y formaron las nubes, y las que cayeron a la tierra formaron ríos, y el tronco formo el grandioso mar.

Desde ese dia los animales tienen con que calmar la séd y disfrutar los beneficios del agua.

"Todos semos dueños del agua debemos cuidarla"

Escrito por: Luis Fernando Hernández

Colombia

LA GOTITA CURIOSA

Escrita por: Pablo Gabriel Zambrano Hernández
Grado: Segundo A
Colegio   Normal Superior Pio XII

En un día no muy caluroso la mamá nube salio de paseo con sus gotitas de agua, había una gotita que era muy curiosa y mientras su mamá saludaba al señor sol, ella bajo por el arcoiris sin permiso de mamá.

La gotita cayó en un campo muy bonito, lleno de flores, mariposas y árboles, ella caminaba y refrescaba todo a su paso, hasta que llego a un rio lleno de malos olores y básura, él le dijo que eso no era nada, que él era su tio y que podría jugar todo lo que quiera la gotita muy curiosa y confiada empezo a jugar con él mientras más jugaba su color fue cambiando, cada vez se volvia más oscura y su olor era muy feo, al darse cuenta de eso la gotita salio corriendo donde sus amigas flores, cuando les conto todo lo ocurrido y las abrazo sus amigos se marchitaron, lo mismo paso con los árboles y el prado, la gotita estaba muy triste por todo el daño que causo, en medio de sus lágrimas miro en el horizonte un globo, ella salío en su búsqueda y cuando lo tomo el globo la llevo nuevamente a su casa, donde su mamá nube.

La mamá nube al mirar a la gotita la regaño por haberse escapado, la gotita pídio disculpas y le explico todo lo ocurrido, mamá nube reunio a las demás nubes y durante todo la noche limpiaron todo el campo con la lluvia

A la mañana siguiente mamá nube y el señor sol se saludaron formando nuevamente el arcoiris y nuestra gotita curiosa volvio a jugar con sus amigos, pero esta vez con permiso de su mamá nube.

trabajo rrealisado por pablo

y FIN

"Bubbles of snow"

Alejandra Chamorro Coral

Colombia

Crystalline water like snow

Indispensable in life

You travel the world without borders

From north to south and from south to north

Through rivers, streams and seas

No one can stop you

By your bubbling fluidity

With strength you glide

Sweeping away what you find in your path

But you are magic, powerful and unreachable

Your great waves fly high

And your noise is breakable to my ears

That's why I become fragile before you.

"Magic Cloud"

Valerie Carbajal Chamorro

Pupiales Colombia

Water is your daily sustenance

Symbol of purity

You generate health and well-being

You are fun you play with the sea

With the sun you reflect flashes of light

When the sun sets

The sun hides

Your innocence calms your flow.

Crystalline water you quench my thirst

You hydrate my body and give us life.

Let us feel committed to the protection of our water.

"THE CLOUDS"

The clouds, playful as usual, seemed to be a group of little kids playing with a ball, but suddenly I saw a word appear before my eyes: GUILT.

Other clouds changed their shape: MOTHER, HELP, PROTECT, HARM... We soon discovered that this was not an isolated phenomenon. Three months nothing had changed.

The wind had stopped blowing, the rain was gone. No cloud lost its white color, no cloud showed any sign of a storm. The weather all over the planet had become uniform.

Crops failed, reservoirs were low, the economy was hanging by a thread and governments were unable to find a solution.

Dozens of experts had been meeting and had only understood that the clouds wanted to convey a message, but were unable to decipher it.

Suddenly, a year later, a cloud changed from pristine white to black. The word that could be read in that cloud was: A. And as if it were a game of dominoes, more clouds became dark as the most infernal night.

Now the message consisted of four words, viz: TO ALL MANKIND.

And the day came when the whole message was discovered. To all mankind:

My poles are melting due to the destruction of the ozone layer, the forests are disappearing thanks to deforestation, hundreds of species are becoming extinct every year and you do not stop accumulating more and more garbage, polluting the oceans and rivers. And not only my rivers suffer, I also breathe in chemical compounds.

I have reached my limit. I have waited for a change, but it has not happened. I am truly sorry, but after waiting for years for a sign of change I see that it is not possible, I have realized: if you want something done right, do it yourself....

The long-awaited rain began to fall. Soon joy turned to terror. The heavens were unloading a year's worth of accumulated rain. All life was swept away and the land was depopulated. Now it could start all over again.

"The crystal waterfall"

Juan David Benavides Vázquez Colombia

Once upon a time there was a beautiful drop of water that lived very happily in the crystal waterfall, every day he walked along its path contemplating the beautiful place, he lived with his great friend the tree that he called "bread stick".

Breadstick from his height watched every day as the drop of water enjoyed the crystal-clear waterfall. And at nightfall it would fall asleep in its leaves, giving it all its energy to survive.

Summer had arrived and palo de pan felt very tired, because the heat of the sun dried his roots and his leaves were carried away by the wind, seeing his great friend so sad he wanted to visit Mr. sun, but he had to go through several places that did not guarantee him to return to his beautiful place, but his friendship was very strong and he had to help palo de pan.

At dawn, without her friend seeing her, she fled. When she arrived at the forest, with great anguish she watched how the fire was destroying large trees and with a loud voice she called Mrs. Rain before the sun came out. Immediately the rain came and extinguished the ravenous fire and so the drop managed to cross the forest and reach the mountain where the sun lived.

Suddenly there was a great avalanche that dragged it towards the outskirts of a city, the drop of water was very disturbed and fell into the pipes of that city, it felt dirty and smelled unpleasant and to make matters worse it was stuck, it felt that it was spoiled with strange things, bottles, food, papers that came from above that place.

From the bottom of the place a voice could be heard saying: - If you want to get out of here you must clean the main door that is over here!

The drop wanted to get to the bottom of the place, but it was impossible to get through. Suddenly a little mouse arrived in search of food and when it looked at the drop it said: - What is such a beautiful drop doing in these places?

She answered: - I came to the crystal waterfall and now I don't know how to go back - Don't be afraid, I will help you.

-Don't be afraid, I will help you," said the little mouse.

The little mouse called all his friends and so they were able to clean that place, they managed to uncover the main door and so the water continued its flow. THE drop was very grateful and invited the mouse to spend a few days at the crystal waterfall, but first she needed to see Mr. Sun so that her breadstick friend would not fall asleep forever. The little mouse took her to the sea which would take her to the eastern mountains.

In the sea she met many little colorful fish that invited her to stay and play with the huge waves and warned her not to go too far out to sea because she could get lost, and the drop let herself be guided in the direction of the current as the sea carried her towards the east.

At the edge of the sea, she saw a huge mountain from which very bright rays were coming out and with joy she headed towards it, but as she got closer, she felt it was melting, and so it melted little by little and now it had become a mass of steam and with great force it reached the clouds where it met more droplets just like it.

From the top he could see his friend palo and together with the friendly clouds decided to help him by making him fall a great refreshment of rain and his friend was happy with a lot of energy, because the water fell and his seeds had germinated, and the crystal waterfall shone with great colors surrounded by beautiful drops.

Now Mr. Sun comes out for short periods and when the forests and rivers feel in trouble, they call the clouds to send droplets of water and everyone can live with great happiness. END

"A visit to the wasteland"

Emily Sofia Enriquez Colombia

Once upon a time there was a boy named Luis and his parents went to visit the páramo de la paja blanca to get to know the frailejones, orchids, chupallas, mortiños, mosses and the different species of flora and fauna of the place. When they reached the top of a mountain, they found a fountain of crystalline water gushing from the mosses and plants on the ground.

Luis was amazed, the three continued walking, Jose the father felt hungry and took some candy out of his backpack that they shared, but they left the garbage on the ground the three irresponsible ones. Fortunately, Alegrin the goblin saw the behavior of the visitors and went to look for the rest of the goblins that lived there.

All the angry goblins planned to teach them a lesson, while the visitors got cold and looked for a dry place to make a fire, and when they lit the fire, it began to spread to a large part of the vegetation.

Everything was burning and the elves saw it and with their magic they provoked rain to come and put out the fire, but not satisfied with this, Leticia, Luis' mother, pulled up plants from the moor to take them to her house as ornaments. All this increased the anger of the goblins and they approached her annoyed by the behavior and were aggressive scaring them and began to scare them away with loud screams, loud laughter and whirlwinds of strong winds of magic, cries and noises.

The frightened visitors descended as best they could from the top of the mountain, while the goblins threw the garbage, they had left at them, asking them to leave without polluting or staining the moor and to take care of the water.

When they descended from the mountain, the goblins disappeared, and Luis and his family began to recover their calm, when they met Mrs. Rosa Aura, protector of the páramo, and in anguish they told her what had happened.

The lady, also upset, called their attention, explaining that the páramo is the main source of water for some communities. And the ways to care for, sustain and conserve the water springs, she told them about reforestation, soil maintenance, protection of flora and fauna species and the entire ecosystem that needs a balance for its proper functioning.

Luis and his parents understood their mistake and since that day they have been doing activities to make people aware of the care of the páramo and the water sources. Making them see that it is a limited resource because it is influenced by the felling of trees, the contamination of rivers and streams, soil intoxication by fungicides from crops, and because people throw garbage and plastics.

Since then, Luis is happy visiting the moors and learning about them and nature to let others know the importance of protecting them so that they also take care of natural resources, especially water.

And that's it, this story is over.

END

Children at the Fray Buenaventura Library in Pupiales Colombia.

Courtesy of teacher Lic. Anna Anna Isabel Cárdenas González

Children of Unique Blossom School Ikorodu-Lagos Nigeria.
Teachers and Headmistress. Ms. Bola Animashaun. March-2021
Courtesy of the Headmistress.

**School in Nepal Hindu Vidyapeeth Nepal
Courtesy of Dr Samrat Natth Yogi Ambassador Worldwide Peace
Organization Nepal.**

Drawings/poems by children from Children's Peace Home (CPH) Nepal for AQUITIN

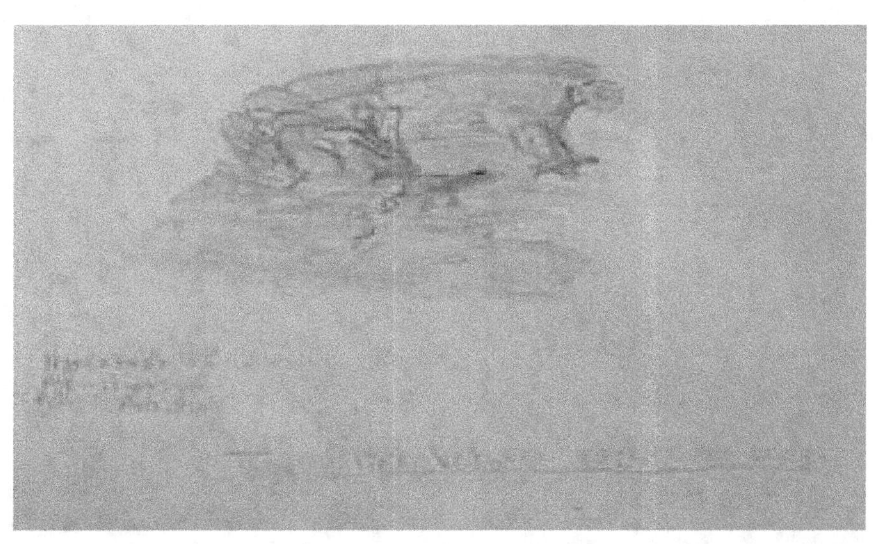

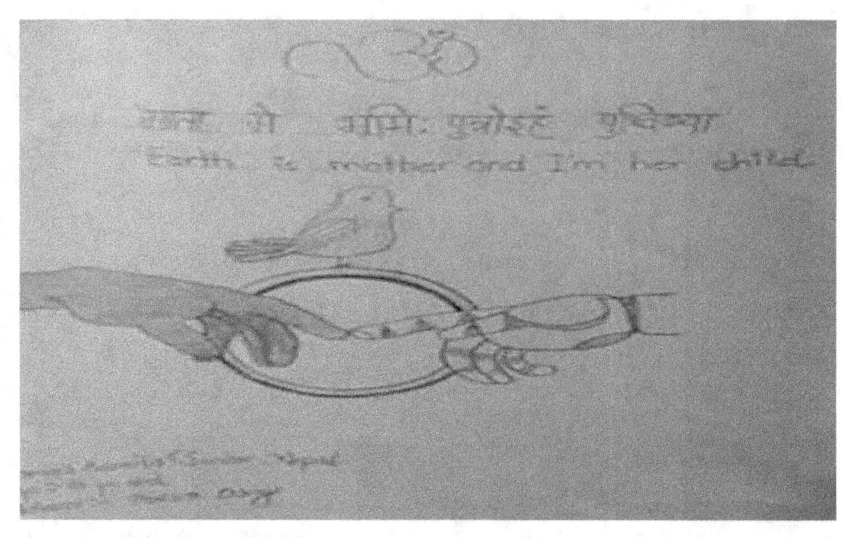
॥ॐ॥
जननी जन्मभूमिश्च स्वर्गादपि गरीयसी
Earth is mother and I'm her child

WINDOW

I heard a bird from my window
Sitting singing on a tree
The roses red and white
and the tailed bird on a tea

Butterflies are flying
[illegible]
and [illegible] the bright sun
over the hills [illegible]

[illegible]
[illegible]
[illegible]
[illegible]

I find the beauty of nature
[illegible]
[illegible]
Shorting point of peace

[illegible]
(Age - Fourteen 14)
[illegible] Dang, Nepal

NATURE

Name - [illegible]
Age - 14(Fourteen)
Address - Dang, Nepal

Our dream is in our nature
Earth is very small but its
beautyness is very greater
We have to make nature better
So we have to use natural
resources in a better resources
Then we be In a good creator......

Nature will be made of peace
Then all living beings be a happy
May there be peace in water!!!
Might there be peace in plants
Bring peace is it that we need......

Earth is our mother
We are her child
For good development of nature
Use our fresh mind
Oh God of water we salute you
Which is source of life
Oh goddess of forest we salute you
Which value is infinite
We save our earth and
earth save our life......

Children's Peace Home (CPH) Children's Peace Home.

(CPH) is an organization based in Dang, western Nepal, run by Dr. Bhola Nath Yogi and his family. For 26 years.

CPH serves orphaned and war-affected children and adolescents, the destitute and homeless children of Nepal, providing them with free education, food and shelter.

Our Magazine supports the work at CPH of our friends' children and youth who receive each issue of our Magazine in Spanish and English so that they also learn and keep updated on environmental issues. They also participate in our International Contest that ends on June 5th.

In addition, they send us their works that we publish as part of this family of Friends of Nature in AQÜITÍN. We also want them to learn our language and meet more children from other continents.

Drawings and poem by Niños en España for this special edition of the magazine.

Laura Orduñez Bologa Age: 12 de Vilanova i la Geltrú 1ro Eso

Instituto: F.X .Lluch i Rafecas

Aitor Buongiovanni 9 years old Sevilla

"The smallest creatures

Daniela María Jorge Monteagudo

God, my God
There is a question I have not asked you
I ask you without complex
Why are there little bugs so even.

When they hear my footsteps
They run scared
I don't understand what happened
And I ask my mother.

Mom answers me
They are afraid, seeing such a huge being
I stand still
To see the little butterfly.

She with many colors
She flutters with love
It lands on my finger
With a lot of sparkle.

An ant passes by
With a little cup with a little sugar
Without ceasing, it takes it to its pretty little house.

Educational Center : IES Puerto del Rosario 3rd ESO

"Forests, water and animals".

Francisco Javier Perez Arreaga . 13 years old.
Federico Mayor Zaragoza Institute. Year 1ESO C.

Hello children!

I'm Bonnie the rabbit. Today we are going to talk about the importance of forests, water and animals like me.

Well, you have to know that forests are fundamental to live, for example they give us fruits and vegetables and they are very cool, you can walk among their trees, camp, climb ... The possibilities are endless! And besides, if we didn't have forests, I wouldn't have a house and I wouldn't have food.

The water is also very important, from it we get food like fish or crabs. You can also swim and play.

Animals are very important. They are not only friendly and playful; they also serve as food. And they are very cute, just like me!

Well kids, what I mean by this is that without these three things, you and I wouldn't exist.

So, take care of nature, recycle, don't throw garbage into the rivers, seas or oceans.

Take care of the animals, remember this throughout your lives because this is very important.

Nature must be taken care of, because if you pollute the water today it may not have a solution, in fact all the fish would die almost instantly, and that's nothing, the animals that drink from it and humans would also die.

Good bye! It was a pleasure to meet you.

Best regards, Bonnie Bunny.
See you later, I hope to see you again very soon, your friend Bonnie the bunny.

For the Friends of Nature. I hope you liked it. "Forests , water and animals".

"MELODI, LA NATURALEZA Y DIOS"

-Érase una vez una niña llamada Melodi que le encantaba la naturaleza, pero los demás la destruían. Melodi estaba cansada de decir que no tiraran basura al suelo.

-¡No tires eso, para algo hay una papelera!- Decía Melodi.

Un día fue al bosque de su pueblo y vio a hombres talando árboles, les dijo que pararan pero ellos ni caso. Entonces Melodi acudió a Dios para que la ayudara y Dios, no respondió, por ahora... Al día siguiente fue a ver el bosque y cuando fue los hombres no estaban y habían más árboles. También cuando fue a la ciudad no había basura por el suelo y se estaban usando más las bicicletas y autobuses ¡Dios hizo un milagro! Desde ese día Melodi le hablaba más a Dios y siempre que hacía algo mal pedía perdón y colorín colorado este cuento se ha acabado.

Noemí Campos 10 años Escuela 4TO PRIMARIA.
CEIP: "Valle De La Osa" Constantina Sevilla
11-04-2021

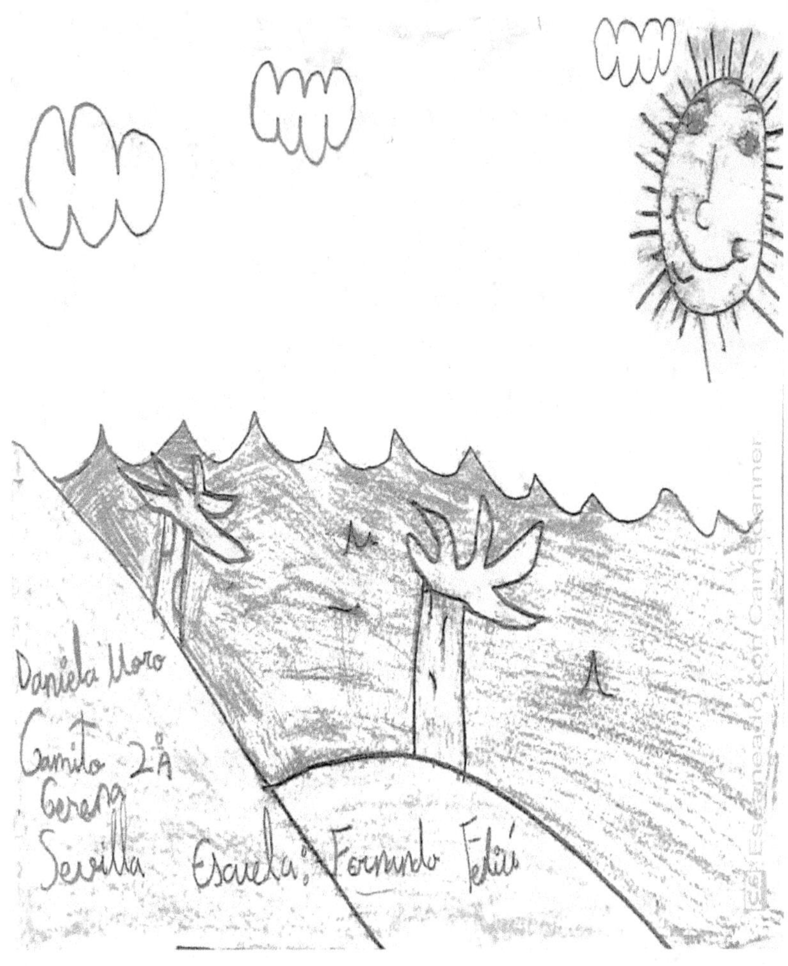

Daniela Moro Gamito Gerena Sevilla

School Fernando Feliu Gerena Seville

"El Niño Y El Bosque"

Había una vez un Maravilloso Bosque había un niño que protegía a los árboles y no le gustaba los animales. Y un día vinieron unos cazadores furtivos y querían cazar a unos animales y el niño le daba igual. Y de pronto le habló una voz del cielo y decía: Tienes que cuidar los animales porque los animales son seres vivos hechos por Mí. Y el niño estaba llorando porque era una señal de Dios, y decidió el niño hacer trampas, no mortales, y escondió todos los animales en un mismo sitio, los cazadores cayeron en todas las trampas y huyeron. Y el niño contento le dice Dios: Hiciste una buena obra y mis ángeles te van a proteger. Y Dios hizo todo esto para que al niño le gustaran los animales.

Fin

Para la REVISTA AGÜITÍN Amigos De La Naturaleza

La Fontanilla 11 de Abril de 2021
Diddier Jalomón González 11 años Sevilla (Utrera)

Section 6 Educational Stories and Poems by Writers for this Exclusive Friends of Nature Edition.

"Friend rain"

Almarí Albarenque 4/04/2021
Teacher and writer. Uruguay

That January afternoon Elsa came home from work hot and tired. Early in the morning she dreamed of taking a bath and having a cool drink in her backyard, under her beloved tree.

Her children had been playing in the pool for hours, swimming fast like fish and racing to see who could get to the opposite end first, while Aunt Dora timed them on her watch. They were free of schedules and enjoyed their summer vacation very much. They liked playing in the water so much that at snack time they had to beg to get out of the water, especially Elias who was always the last to go to snack.

On the other side of the border in a beautiful country called Brazil, more precisely in the State of Ceará, the situation was very different. Pedro lived there and wondered anxiously when it would rain again. He and his neighbors prayed daily for rain so that their crops would not perish again because of the great drought, for it seemed that the friendly rain had forgotten them.

It so happens that the land is so large that in some places water is abundant and flows quickly even when turning on a faucet, but in others it is so scarce that everyone has to walk several kilometers carrying buckets to get a little water so that they can drink, cook and bathe.

Julieta listened very attentively to her aunt Dora's interesting story, her siblings had already fallen asleep, but she always liked to know how people live in other places on planet earth. She imagined how those people, animals and plants could live with so little water at their disposal and felt sorry for them. Their life was so different! She was used to her friend rain visiting her often.

In her little country called Uruguay, the pastures were almost always green, the country animals could bathe in the streams and everything bloomed in spring. For those who lived on the outskirts of the city, it was common to hear the toads singing in the ditches, announcing the arrival of her friend.

That week she was looking forward to Sunday, because that day her cousins were coming for lunch and then they would have a fun "Water Guerrilla", their favorite summer game.

She asked her aunt what she could do to help take care of the water and promised to implement some of her ideas; for example, she would make her daily bath not last more than ten minutes; she would also turn off the faucet while she brushed her teeth and what she found most difficult: she would propose to her siblings and cousins to suspend the Water Guerrilla, since they would still have a lot of fun playing in the pool.

Juliet kept her promise; she talked to her siblings first, but they didn't like the idea very much. Even so, she did not give up and when Sunday arrived, she did so with her cousins; to her surprise, they did agree to suspend the game.

Her grandparents were surprised and very happy to learn of her changes in her attitude to save water, and congratulated her since by doing so she would be collaborating with the wellbeing of many beings.

Her aunt Dora hugged her very tightly and gave her two kisses on each cheek. Her siblings and cousins, observing all this, decided to imitate her. Perhaps if they all collaborated, even a little, others could enjoy this great treasure without having to make so many sacrifices.

"The tree of wisdom".

Lic. María Cristina Azcona
Writer Buenos Aires Argentina

In the land forgotten by all

The tree of wisdom grows.

It waits for the enlightened mind

Of some children will one day discover it.

When this happens, a way will open

And all will be able to see its golden light.

Even where drought reigns.

Near the confines of nothingness.

The flower of consciousness will awaken

In the soul that is still asleep

When it feels the perfume of its knowledge.

For knowledge gives new life

To mankind who in vain ignorance

Believes that the truth is already known.

"A drop of water: a stream of hope".

Dr Illeana Martínez Cabrera
Spanish Scientist 27-3-2021

Little friend. I will not tell you a tale of dragons, nor of glaciations. I will show you what a drop of water is worth in the islands.

If you live in a large country in extension, the chances of finding rivers, streams and lakes, may be really advantageous because the large clouds coming from other areas are sources of precipitation and water will be better preserved in these aquiferous lands.

I will tell you what was narrated to me by a little drop of water that came in a heavy rain and stayed on my clothes before reaching land.

On islands like the one I live on, where there are no rivers, no ponds, no large lakes; when rain falls a small part of it accumulates in the form of floods. Some gush directly from a small hole between rocks, forming the so-called springs. These spring up once a year when, on certain days, the groundwater is enriched. Unfortunately, on small islands, these springs soon flow into the sea.

The droplet told me that once in the sea, it may evaporate; however, the clouds could move to other distant areas.

If you live on an island, what water sources would you use for drinking?

On many islands where there are no large natural water supplies, there are water purifiers, intended for external use, such as washing dishes, clothes.

To drink, the droplet must come in containers of water coming from distant places, in boats.

This is why, for those of us who live on islands, water is so important. It is so important that it rains in the seasons when rain should be abundant.

If you are up for it, look at the rivers in your town. Watch the ducks. And if you have the sea nearby, look for ducks too. These animals can swim and live in places with both types of water. Their bodies are prepared for it.

We, too, can swim in both places; but to do so, we must take care of their cleanliness.

The droplet said goodbye to me very soon, because the ambient temperature made it evaporate again. But it promised to come back and we agreed to do so.

There will always be a stream of hope for a droplet to join it, greet us and tell us more of what the whole world is doing so that the droplet, when it falls, finds its cycle without problems.

"Nepaja laguna rescued".

María del Socorro Rodríguez.
Managua, Nicaragua. 29/03/2021

On the other side of the Atlantic Ocean, there is a sister country, Nicaragua, which has a lagoon of volcanic origin, called Nejapa.

It is not inhabited by many animals, because it has been cleared of its environment and dries up in summer. But for the joy of people who like animals, there survive two turtles, twin brothers, orphans, Paco and Freckles, 10 years old, they love each other very much and are kind. They are survivors, because in summer they live in a small pool of water, which only provides them with oxygen, it is like a kind of hibernator.

Paco has a slightly elongated body, bulging eyes and a deep gaze, brown shell and green lamoso, he will be a good boy and Freckles, the older sister, because she broke, first, her egg; her shell is round and shiny brown, with romantic eyes, small mouth, pretty. They both share a secret, what do you think, the secret is that they are foodies and crabs, seaweed and tender herbs or roots are scarce, in times of food crisis. A problem is looming, in summer the lagoon dries up until winter when the water recovers a little.

For this reason, they talk about it: Freckles, what shall we do, so that the lagoon does not lose its water this summer and we have enough to drink, eat, swim and live without worries.

-We will join Hugo, the lagoon guard, to give us some seeds and plant them, because we need to plant trees, since "Trees provide us with oxygen, shade, fruits, beauty, environmental harmony, healthy and balanced life, and facilitate the generation of water".

-So, let's plant trees," said Paco. -So, they did, they got the bags of seeds and hung them around their necks, got out of the water and climbed some 300 meters up the slope of the lagoon. The interesting thing about this initiative is that, although it was very difficult for them to carry it out, they always had a positive and successful attitude. And, when they were sowing the seeds, suddenly, they felt a lot of humidity and Pecas said _ Paco, here is something that sounds wonderful to me, _ what could it be, Pecas _ asked Paco _ and they called Hugo and told him about the discovery and he, very excited, shouted:

Yes, it looks like something phenomenal and then, all excited, they shout in unison: "WATER", "water", water is wonderful, it means life, health, longevity, love", and they continue digging and digging and to their surprise, they discover an eye of water, which is a great subway source.

Freckles was tired, because her little legs are short and she has to make a lot of effort, but so they continued working. It was a day of hard work, but also of much rejoicing and profit for the future. Paco, Freckles, Hugo and other lake guards joined forces in a single fist and managed to suck and direct the water, through a channel they built, to the lagoon, feeding it with pure, fresh water and it never dried up again.

Days later, they continued planting the seeds of guava, jocote and nancite, so that there would always be freshness and the Nejapa lagoon would not suffer so much from the ravages of climate change. And they commented, we must take care and protect the trees and water, because they nourish our lives.

They were happy and content for the duty accomplished. The Nejapa Lagoon smiled, grateful and proud, to Paco, Pecas and Hugo, for taking care of it and protecting it.

END.

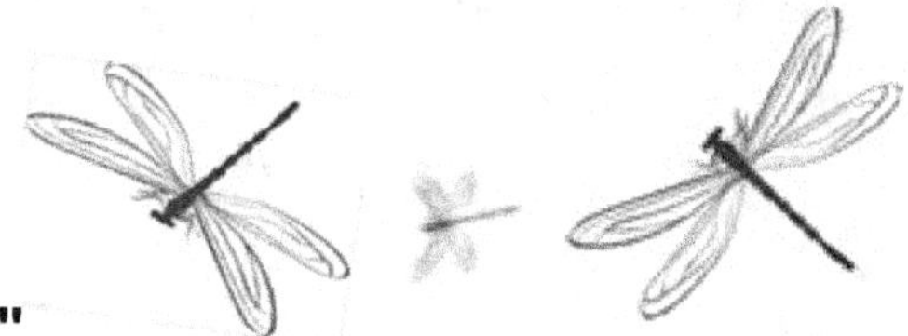

"CEREMONY"

Yolanda F. Rodríguez Toledo
Cuban Writer

Cactus and ferns

in the morning.

Rain falls

frogs jump.

Balls of fire

in the eyes:

Cigarettes

iron their wings.

Reds, blues,

they rise and fall,

like little airplanes

skim the water.

Last flight,

the larvae sleep

under the mirror

next to my house.

"The rain, the kiss and the Mainnumby".

Gladys Mercedes Writer from Goya, Argentina.

There are days when rain is not a simple rain. There are days when the water falls to earth dragging thoughts, dreams and different missions. Then the rain comes out of its lethargy, stops being asleep and sounds on the roofs, in the chest of men and becomes a visible hero, a tender giant who bends down to wake up the flower of the kiss from the long road of eternity. Thus, the rain and the kiss permeate each other, become one, a single dream, a single awakening. A fusion of souls is prepared, while outside suddenly all is silence. The flower of the kiss is ready for its journey on earth, ready with its velvet nectar to receive its beloved, its mainumby.

Every being on earth has its mainumby, its half. Their unique soul nectar connection. Once chosen, that flowerpecker will be faithful to its flower until eternity and will become territorial and will defend it from other birds, from other beings that want to delight in its kisses. Such is the sacred union of the flower of El Beso and the mainunby. The rain knows it and has come down that morning of all the mornings to come to awaken".

Ilustration Gladys Mercedes Acevedo

"THE ANTS THAT STUDIED".

Dr Juan David Romero Arboleda
Writer Cali Colombia.

The queen of the ants,
asks the others,
who wants to be queen?
or General.

And a few of them
raised their little hand,
one who had glasses,
another who was petite.

The others just wanted
to be part of the anthill,
they just wanted to carry,
walking very lightly.

And those two little ants,
they did different jobs
they would stay up all night long,
to achieve their promotions.

While the other ones
happily made merry,
drank flower nectar,
and ran through the forest.

Then the course ended,
and there was a sincere homage
they graduated with honors,
first of all, the anthill.

Now some time has passed,
they ask each other
why, being so equal,
they were the brutes.

And they walk all day long,
carrying heavy loads,
while Chiqui and Gafitas,
Lead the long march.

They deny bad fortune
for not having studied,
they go through the burning dunes,
marching like soldiers.

The lesson is:

To get ahead
And be able to succeed
You have to study hard
And work very hard.

"Gifts from the forest"

Euda Morales Writer
Journalist- Guatemala

-Papi, when will the rains start this year? We are still in the country's dry season, but are there that many days? But, are there so many days? Yes, since the rains start in April; although I know why you ask and then we will have to wait for June... Every time of the year is important and necessary for nature.

I want it to rain to go for a walk in the mountains and you know it will be to find the gifts of the forest. We will be patient, while we go to the market to buy a basket for you.

Last night it rained and today it was sunny, a few more days of rain and we will be ready to go on our tour. -Sarita, you must go to bed early, tomorrow we will wake up at dawn to start the long-awaited tour.

It's time to get up! But look at me, you will see that I am dressed and with the basket in my hands. Perfect, we'll leave now. I am 8 years old, but since I was 4 years old I have accompanied my father, so I remember the path very well and I will be able to find the precious mushrooms. The path is defined, but it is necessary to know where to walk. I look in the trunks or on the ground or off the path, I am happy and sure that I will fill my basket.

-Daddy, why are they called gifts of the forest? Daughter, they are so named because each mushroom is born by itself without having been sown. This is how Amanita caesarea mushrooms, known in the country as San Juan, Q'atzuy or Kantzu mushrooms, or other species such as the orange or blue sharas, during the rainy season, delight the eye with their colorfulness and the palate with their delicate flavor.

-At what age did you start coming to the mountains? I was 6 years old and accompanied your grandfather, who told me that his father was a mushroom hunter and had all the knowledge to recognize the species that could be eaten. This knowledge as well as the love for nature is important and has been transmitted from parents to children as I do with you.

The essential rule is to start the tour in the early hours of the day. In addition, it is necessary to recognize the edible mushrooms, since, during the tour, you will find several varieties, but only a few that can be consumed. The shape is important because when the mushroom is young it has a round cap, but this flattens as it matures. When they sprout the color is red and then yellow or orange when they are ripe and have a golden yellow foot. -Daddy, I've noticed that sometimes you even smell them to be absolutely sure that they are edible.

What happiness! We found quite a few mushrooms and my basket is full. Mom welcomes us and counts 12 mushrooms.

It is essential to eat well, these mushrooms offer a high protein content, are rich in minerals and vitamins - it is always recommended to eat them fresh or keep them for a couple of days.

Today I will cook 6 mushrooms for lunch, it is simple, roasted on the comal, perfumed with lemon drops and seasoned with salt. The rest we will prepare them in a stew and invite the grandparents. Without further ado, they are majestic and have a supreme flavor.

"Like two drops of water".

Professor Norge Sánchez Fonseca Cuba-Venezuela
(Excerpt from the children's novel La bolsaita de caramelo)

- Hey, how pretty you are! And what are you doing here flying so high?

-Well, I'm having fun. Just like you.

-No. I'm not having fun. I'm flying into the upper layers of the atmosphere.

- So why do you have to go so high?

-I'll tell you. I, with all my family, lived in a volcano and from there we were expelled to go to the top of the sky.

-So, it's true what they say about volcanoes.

- And what have you heard about volcanoes?

-Well, that they are aggressive monsters that cover everything with very hot lava and destroy forests and cities.

-It's true that sometimes they overflow and cover the vegetation. But when all that material cools down, it leaves men with an excellent soil for agriculture and nature with a new fertile layer for trees, flowers and fruits to grow again.

- What about the people who destroy?

-It is not the volcanoes' fault. They don't have legs to move. Men can move, but they are stubborn, they build their houses in the wrong places.

-Oh, gee, then volcanoes are good and bad.

-I told you. It depends on how you want to look at it. Look how far he sends us to help nature. And you, where do you come from?

-Well, I used to live in the tires of an elegant automobile, one of those many that can be seen in every city. Do you know them?

-Yes, of course. Everyone talks about them. Some say they are highly polluting. Fossil fuel burners, say others. Others say they are being underutilized. But the reality is that in modern life they are a great friend of civilization.

-That's true. From the asphalt of the roads and highways, from the exhausts of burned fuel and from all the dust that is dispersed on the roads, there are millions of particles that, like me, fly through the air.

-And they affect people's breathing.

- Ah! But that is not our intention.

- What is that intention then?

-Nothing in particular. To go around the world having fun.

-Then I'll do you one better. You come with me and when we're high up, the steam will stick to us as if it wanted to tuck us in.

- What if that humidity gives me the flu?

-No, don't worry, even surrounded by the humid vapor, we'll continue to climb until we become drops of water.

- A water droplet? I'm coming from a speeding tire on a freeway, can I become a water droplet?

-Yes, and when you start to get fat, you will be so heavy that the wind will not be able to hold you up. And of course, because of the law of gravity, we'll fall.

-You're telling me we can become rain. Be part of a downpour?

- Of course, we can! That's the idea. We will be rain if we manage to stay in the tropical regions where the sun's rays maintain high temperatures all year round. But if the winds bring us closer to the polar regions, then we will fall as snow or snow water.

-A no. I want to be rain. I like better the greenery of the forests and the crystal of the streams and rivers that flow day and night to meet the sea.

-Then hurry up. Give me your hand. Come, let's go in search of the heights, that's our best destination together.

-Let's go. She said visibly excited and holding hands they continued towards the heights with the mutual sensation that they had always been great friends and from this moment on their existence would be linked forever.

"The forests of my land".

Professor Anna Isabel Cárdenas González
Pupiales Colombia

The forests of my land, are leafy and slender, with diverse aromas, but at the same time together they are flashes of pleasant aromas to all well the beautiful pines, the grandiose eucalyptus harmonize in great forests and diverse ways in curved, straight lines and kicks that incite the walk...And parallel that incite the walk....

Ahh what a beautiful landscape, that fills the lungs with pure air and great energies to the Being.

What a great gift God has given us, the light of the radiant sun passes through its branches. The luminous rays renew your energy, give you hope for a better tomorrow. When you close your eyes, you feel yourself floating in an earthly paradise, you are filled with its strength and power to be able to continue?

Entering these forests, you are born again and you understand that you are part of the wonders of nature; they catch you to be reborn.

The joy is to be able to contemplate it, to enjoy it, to take care of it and not to harm it.

"YES, FOR A PERFECT WORLD"

Dr Ashok Chakravarthy Tholana
Telangana State, INDIA.

Having pounded the surface and sea,

Having punctured the sky and space,

Having destructed the dense forests,

Having intruded the high mountains;

We have peeled natures unbound beauty

We have devastated invaluable resources,

We have polluted the life-giving air,

We have spoilt the pure water resources.

We have invaded all living species,

We have infiltrated the green valleys,

We have played havoc with rare birds,

We have hunted down the rarest animals.

We have almost inflicted a death blow,

Dear! Yet some hope exists even now,

Ignorance of any sort at this juncture

Shall turn the tide against the universe.

With perfect care and perfect concern,

With perfect word and perfect action,

Let us act perfect, for a future perfect

In a perfect way, yes, for a perfect world.

"INFANCY"

Nélida Baigorria
Mar del Plata-Buenos Aires Argentina

Last night I dreamed I was dreaming

With green fields and children playing.

With shining sidewalks

and ladies chatting.

With open doors.

With clean irrigation ditches

and crystal-clear water,

where my little girl's face is reflected.

But I am not alone, I have company.

As if we were running along with the water.

The weeping tree stares and stares,

receiving thirsty, its vital food.

Leafy tree my faithful companion,

firm component of the living lung,

of my old and distant neighborhood.

Today I wake up confused.

I don't know, if I dreamed while asleep or awake, I remembered

the childhood I lived.

Brief Review of the Contributing Writers of this Issue of the Journal:

■Prof. Emeritus Dr. Ernesto Kahan.
Physician, poet, honorary doctor of literature Faculty of Medicine. Tel Aviv Univ. Israel.
Honorary Academician - Royal European Academy of Doctors. Editorial Board. Honorary Academician - International Academy of Science, Technology, Education and Humanities (AICTEH) Spain. Honorary Academician - American Academy of Modern Literature International (ANLMI).
1st Vice-President of the World Academy of Art and Culture - World Congress of Poets (UNESCO).
Member of the General Association of Writers of Israel. Honorary President of AIELC- Israeli Association of Writers in the Spanish Language. President ISRAEL IPPNW - International Physicians for the Prevention of Nuclear War - IPPNW and delegate to the 1985 Nobel Peace Prize ceremony to IPPNW.
Schweitzer Peace Prize "For courageous action for peace in the Middle East".
Vice President-IFLAC - International Forum for Literature and Culture of Peace.
Honorary President of SIPEA - International Society of Poets, Writers and Artists.
Member of Honor Instituto Vallejiano Universidad Nacional Trujillo - Peru. World Wide Peace Organization WWPO Honorary Founding President.
Founding Member, International Circle of Narrators and Poets of Mercosur. Director of OME - World Writers Organization. 18 books published

■Almarí Albarenque
Prof.: Educator specialized in underprivileged population.
Poetry and narrative writer.
Playwright. Born in Uruguay.

■Almarí Albarenque
Prof.: Educator specialized in underprivileged population.
Poetry and narrative writer.
Playwright. Born in Uruguay.

■Gladys Mercedes Acevedo
Novelist, short story writer, essayist, cartoonist and plastic artist. Born in Goya. Author of novels Curuzú, La rebelión de los infieles and Las Tres Muertes de Camila. Founder of the Museo Gauchesco Cueuzu and the Museo de Mitos y Leyendas Guaraníes. President of the World Association of Latin American Writers. Ambassador of Peace for Argentina appointed in Spain and Switzerland. Founder of the Los Museos Vamos Program (traveling museum) that reaches schools and isolated places.

■Ileana Martínez Cabrera
Degree in Biochemistry and PhD in Pharmaceutical Sciences from the University of Havana. She worked as a teacher at the Faculty of Biology (UH) and at the National Vaccine Institute Finlay. She worked at the Mateu Orfila Foundation (currently Foundation for Health Research of the Balearic Islands, Spain). Master in Clinical Trials Seville. Author of more than 21 scientific publications, one testimonial book and one in press for publication.

■Anna Isabel Cárdenas González.
Teacher and cultural manager of the municipality of Pupiales. With a trajectory of 33 years committed to strengthening culture in its various dimensions and the development of literature and ecology with elementary school children." LITERARY AND ECOLOGICAL SEEDBED CRADLE OF THOUGHT "

■María del Socorro Rodríguez. (Almallanera).
Born in Bluefields-Nicaragua. Retired university professor. Co-author of two published university academic books: Language and Communication I and II. (2009). Virtual poetic publications. Founding President of

UNILETRAS-Nicaragua. Member of Unión Hispanomundial Escritores (UHE).

■Yolanda Felicita Rodríguez Toledo
Licentiate in Sociocultural Studies. Writer and Plastic Artist. Literary Specialist and Member of the Council of Specialized Readers Editorial Luminaria, Cuba. Her work appears in various periodicals and Literary Magazines in Cuba and abroad, such as: La Pedrada, Matanzas, Ariel, Chinchila, El tintero; Spanish magazine Amigos de la poesía de Castellón; and in the Magazine of Spanish-speaking writers, published in Cagua, Venezuela: Letralia, Tierra de Letras.

■Juan David Romero Arboleda
Law Degree
Dr Odontology. Colombian poet and fabulist.
He has more than four hundred fables to his credit. Writer of children's and young people's poetry. Tithes and hymns.

■Eduardo Reyes Escudero
Originally from Tetela del Volcán, Morelos, currently in San Andrés Tuxtla, Veracruz, Mexico. Public School Academic Teacher. Primary Level.
Painter, Muralist. Illustrator Special Edition Friends of Nature Special Edition Environmental Educational Magazine of Water and Nature for children AQÜITÍN 2021.

■ María Cristina Azcona
Buenos Aires. Argentina. Psychopedagogue and Family Counselor. Psychopedagogue by the University USAL of Buenos Aires, Argentina, 1975.
Family Counselor, University of Navarra, Spain, 1999.
National Normal Teacher, Colegio Mallinckrodt, Martinez, Buenos Aires, Argentina, 1999. Senior English Teacher, English Cultural Academy, Olivos, Buenos Aires, Argentina.
Academic member in the area of Education of the Center for the Study of Dignity and Humiliation, Columbia University, USA.
https://www.humiliationstudies.org/whoweare/coreteamlong.php#azcona
Writer, Poet, Prologist and Lecturer. For Peace and Culture.
Author of books in several languages and Anthologies.

President of Worldwide Peace Organization (Wwpo) and Paz-iflac Peace Ambassador of the Swiss and French Peace Ambassadors Circle International Board Member at IAWEP International Educators for Peace USA.

■Manuel Garrocho Escobar
Born in Morón de la Frontera Seville 1962, Painter since childhood. Self-taught. Specialty. Realism. Portraits and Landscape. Social painting highlighting the needy. Diverse techniques. Charcoal and different techniques. Effective use of mixtures of pigments and oil essences.

■Norge Sánchez Fonseca
(Cuba, 1958). Narrator, poet and editor.
University professor. He has published in Cuba, Venezuela and the United States of America more than twenty books of poetry, novels, testimonies, short stories and a wide range of literature for children and young people. His texts appear in magazines and newspapers in several countries.

■Dr. Ashok Chakravarthy Tholana
Writer, poet and reviewer, hailing from Hyderabad City, Telangana State, INDIA. During his 30-year stint with poetry, Ashok's message-oriented poems have the rare distinction of getting published in no less than 90 countries. Gladys Mercedes Acevedo
Novelist, short story writer, essayist, cartoonist and plastic artist. Born in Goya. Author of novels Curuzú, La rebelión de los infieles and Las Tres Muertes de Camila. Founder of the Museo Gauchesco Cueuzu and the Museo de Mitos y Leyendas Guaraníes. President of the World Association of Latin American Writers. Ambassador of Peace for Argentina appointed in Spain and Switzerland. Founder of the Los Museos Vamos Program (traveling museum) that reaches schools and isolated places.

■Dr. Ashok Chakravarthy Tholana
Writer, poet and reviewer, hailing from Hyderabad City, Telangana State, INDIA. During his 30-year stint with poetry, Ashok's message-oriented poems have the rare distinction of getting published in no less than 90 countries.
Relentlessly he is contributing poetry concentrating on themes for promoting Universal Peace, World Brotherhood, Environment

Consciousness, Protection of Nature, Safeguarding Children's and Human Rights, uplifting the oppressed-downtrodden etc. For his outstanding contribution and promotion of world literature and culture, he is conferred prestigious national and international FIVE Doctorates, lots of laurels.

In recognition of his poetry writings, received commendations from Dr. APJ Abdul Kalam, former-President, India, Shri Atal Behari Vajpayee, former-Prime Minister, India, Bill Clinton, USA, Queen Elizabeth of Britain, Princess of Wales, President and Prime Minister of France, Prime Minister of Switzerland, Senator Viktor Busa, The Lord President, Italy, United Nationals Organization, UNESCO, UNICEF etc.

■Bola Animashaun
B.A. English and Education at University of Lagos, Nigeria.
Lawyer and Lecturer in communication skills for 10 years at Federal College of Education (Technical) Akoka - Lagos Nigeria.
Headmistress of Unique Blossom School, ikorodu - Lagos.
Nursery and elementary school. From 18 months to 11 years old.

■Nélida Baigorria

Mar del Plata - Buenos Aires Argentina Writer, Poet and Plastic Artist - Ambassador of Peace International Forum for a Literature and Culture of PEACE IFLAC and Organization for World PEACE - Delegate for "IFLAC" in Cities of the Coast of Buenos Aires Argentina.

Producer and Conductor of the Program "NO ME SUELTES" Radio-TV. Literary Cultural Coordinator of "Great Women of the World for Peace" 2018 - 2019 - Organizer of the Meeting "Chain of men and women for PEACE" in Cabildo de Mar del Plata Argentina 2019 Author of books: "LISTEN TO MY HEART, "VIRTUAL LOVE, and more than 20 Anthologies: Publication of poems in Magazine Turkish Literature 2017 - Publication in "Magazine Zas" Madrid: "History of the Library Alma Fuerte" La Plata - Buenos Aires - Argentina.

■Dr. Bhola Nath Yogi.
Founder Director of Vidyapeeth Hindu School, in Dang School for day children. For three decades serving the underprivileged society and the needy. Social worker and Director of old age home.

Dir Disabled Association of Nepal and Care center for children with Down syndrome.
Dr.BholaNath Yogi bholacph@gmail.com

Website: http://peaceserviceusa.org/ For collaborations help we indicate the mails. Dr. Chintamani Yogi mail2cmyogi@yahoo.com

■Dr. Chintamani Yogi
Founding director of the Vidyapeeth Hindu School in Kathmandu. He is a spiritual teacher, religious leader and a great motivator.
He is the founder of the Peace Service Center in Kathmandu. As a social worker, he has also been serving the society since many decades.
Director of old age home. Dir Disabled Association of Nepal Dir Care Center for children with Down Syndrome.

BIBLIOGRAPHY

- NEWSLETTER AQUAE Foundation. 2021

-Environment Outlook 2020. UNEP. Ed. Mundi.

- Vivendi Environment. Annual Report 2000.

- nationalgeographic.com

- Organic Vegetable Garden TIPS PLANTS TIPS Organic Vegetable Garden

- 28 September, 2017 by Maria Bilobrowka

- Organización de las Naciones Unidas para la Alimentación y la Agricultura,ONUAA, FAO(por sus siglas en inglés: *Food and Agriculture Organization*),